Bridgestone
BOOKS

Earthforms

Rivers

by Kay Jackson

Consultant:
John D. Vitek
Assistant Dean of Graduate Studies
Texas A & M University
College Station, Texas

Capstone press

Mankato, Minnesota

What Are Rivers?

Wide or narrow, slow or fast, a river is water moving through a **channel**. Smaller channels, called creeks and streams, combine to form a river.

A river takes **freshwater** from its **source**, or beginning, to its end, or **mouth**. A river's banks hold the water as it moves to an ocean, a lake, or another river.

◀ The Jökulsá á Brú River in Iceland flows quickly between rocky, grass-covered banks.

source

OCEAN

mouth

How Do Rivers Form?

Rivers begin on tall mountains and hills. Water from melting **glaciers**, snow, and rain trickles into creeks. Rain runs over rocks into little streams.

Water near a river's source moves fast. It rushes down a mountain or hill. The water slows down as it reaches the bottom. As creeks and streams meet, they form a river. The river curves across the land. At the mouth, a river widens. The water flows into an ocean, a lake, or another river.

◀ Water from creeks and streams combines to form a river. The river widens at its mouth and joins the ocean.

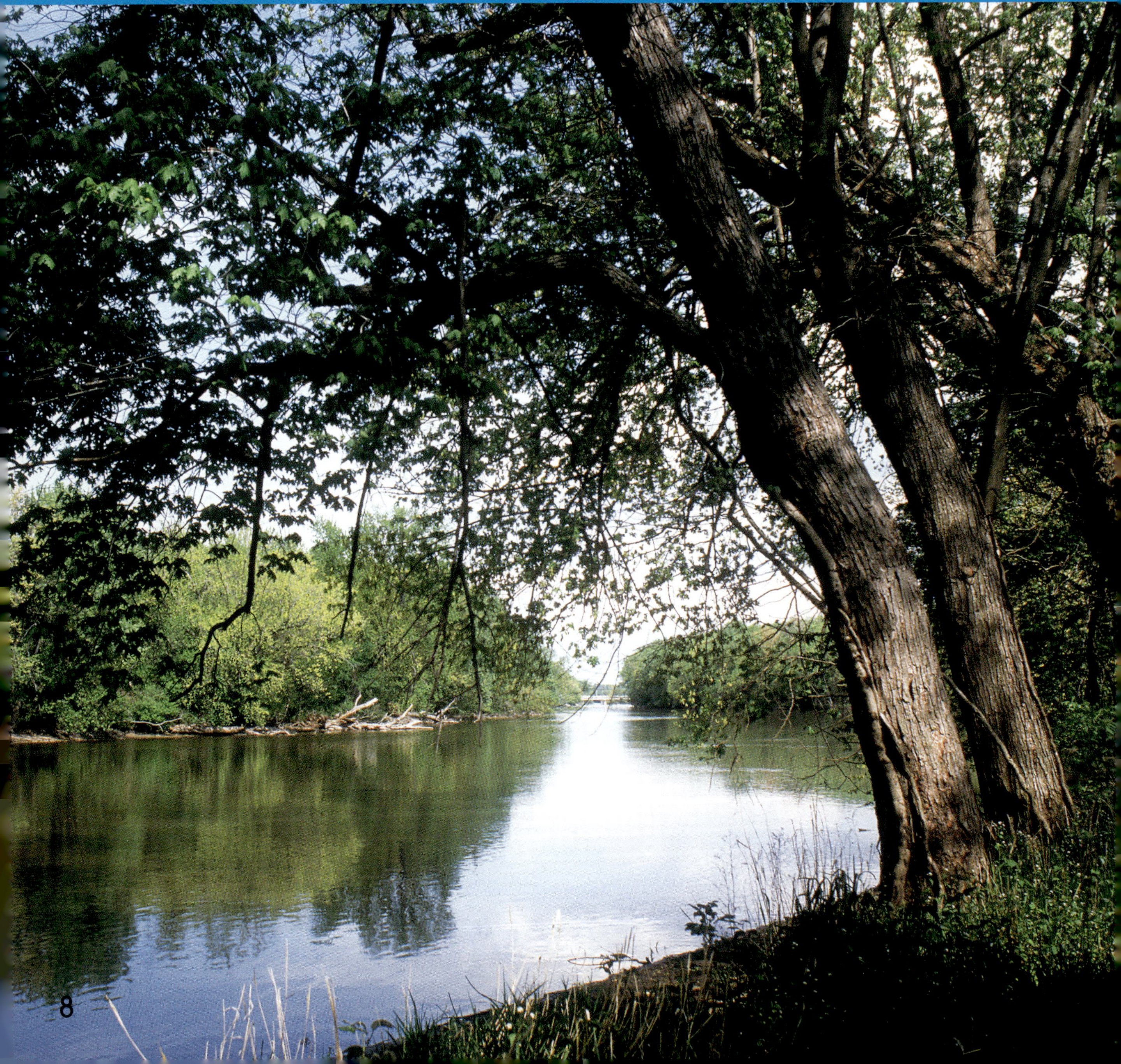

River Plants

Climate affects which plants can grow in and along rivers. A river's water temperature is determined by climate. Plants that grow along cold rivers are very different from plants near warm river waters.

In cold rivers, soft ferns and mosses cling to rocks. Tall pine trees drop cones beside the clear waters.

Along warm rivers, willow and oak trees shade the water. Grasses line the banks. In spring, thistles bloom near the water.

◀ Trees and grass cover the banks of the warm Rock River as it flows through Wisconsin and Illinois.

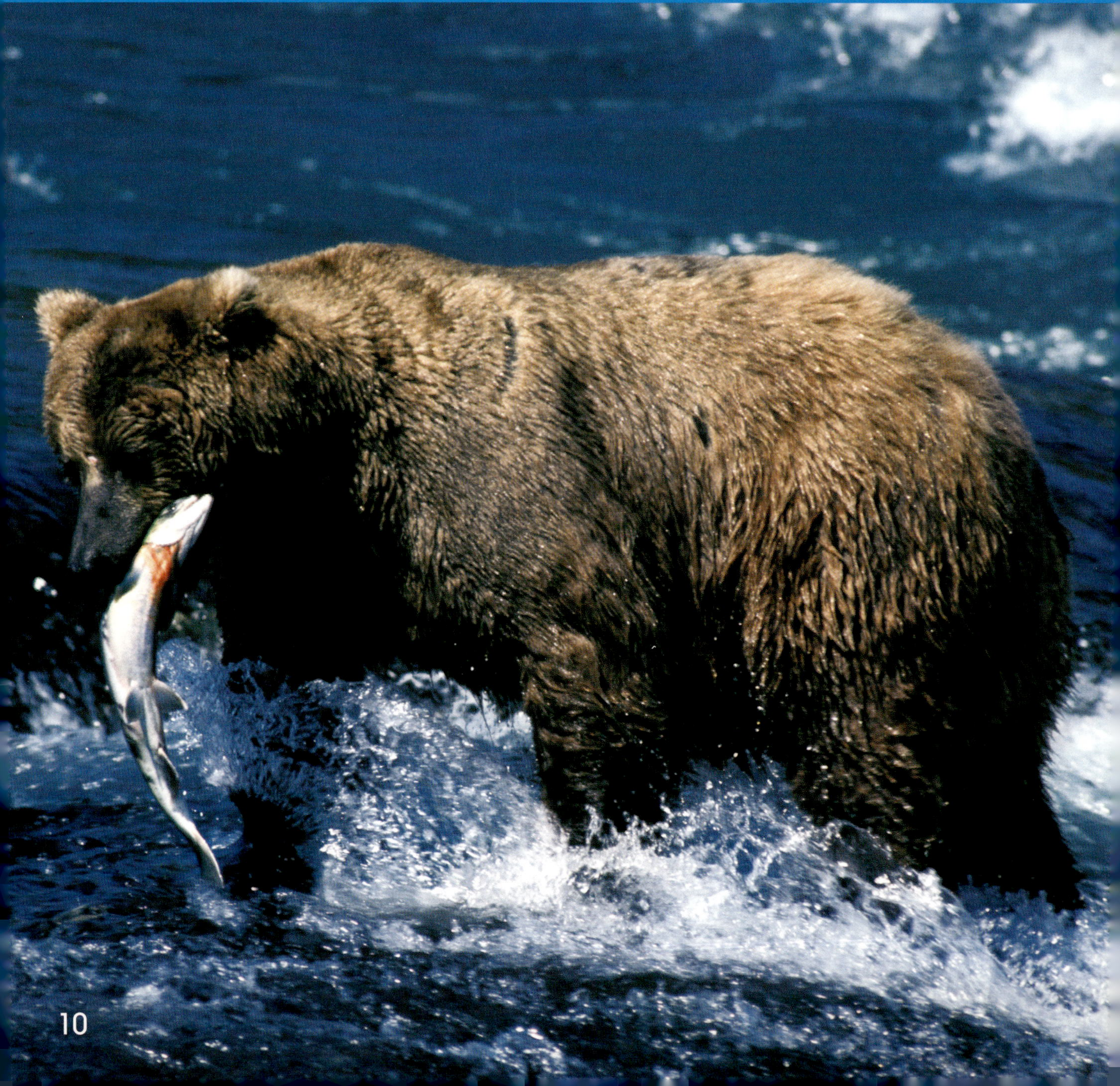

River Animals

Climate also affects which animals live in and around rivers. Many animals live in and near warm rivers. Blue kingfishers swoop down and grab small silverfish. On sandy banks, bullfrogs snap up dragonflies. In Africa, crocodiles float in the Nile River.

Fewer animals live near cold rivers. Bears and eagles grab salmon from the chilly water. Beavers use tree branches to build **dams** across rivers.

◂ A hungry grizzly bear catches a salmon in Alaska's McNeil River.

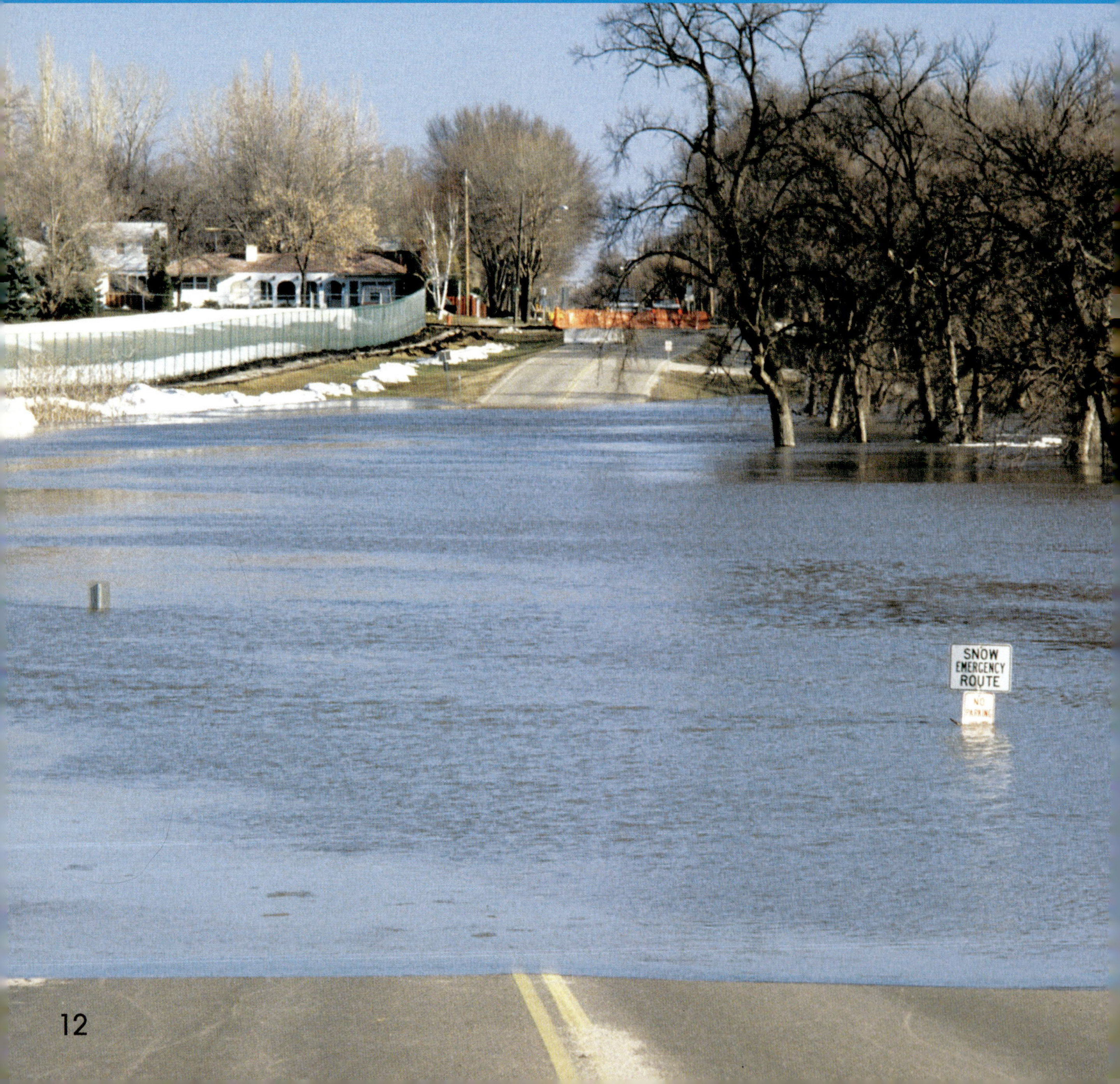
SNOW
EMERGENCY
ROUTE

Weather Changes Rivers

Weather changes the size of a river. A tiny river can become huge when rain and snow add to it. Too much water can make rivers overflow their banks and cause floods. In the spring and summer, rivers often flood. During dry weather, rivers can be shallow and slow.

A river's speed can be quickly changed by the weather. In winter, huge ice chunks slow rivers' flows. In spring, warm temperatures melt the ice, and rivers run fast again.

◀ The Red River bursts out of its banks, flooding the city streets of Fargo, North Dakota.

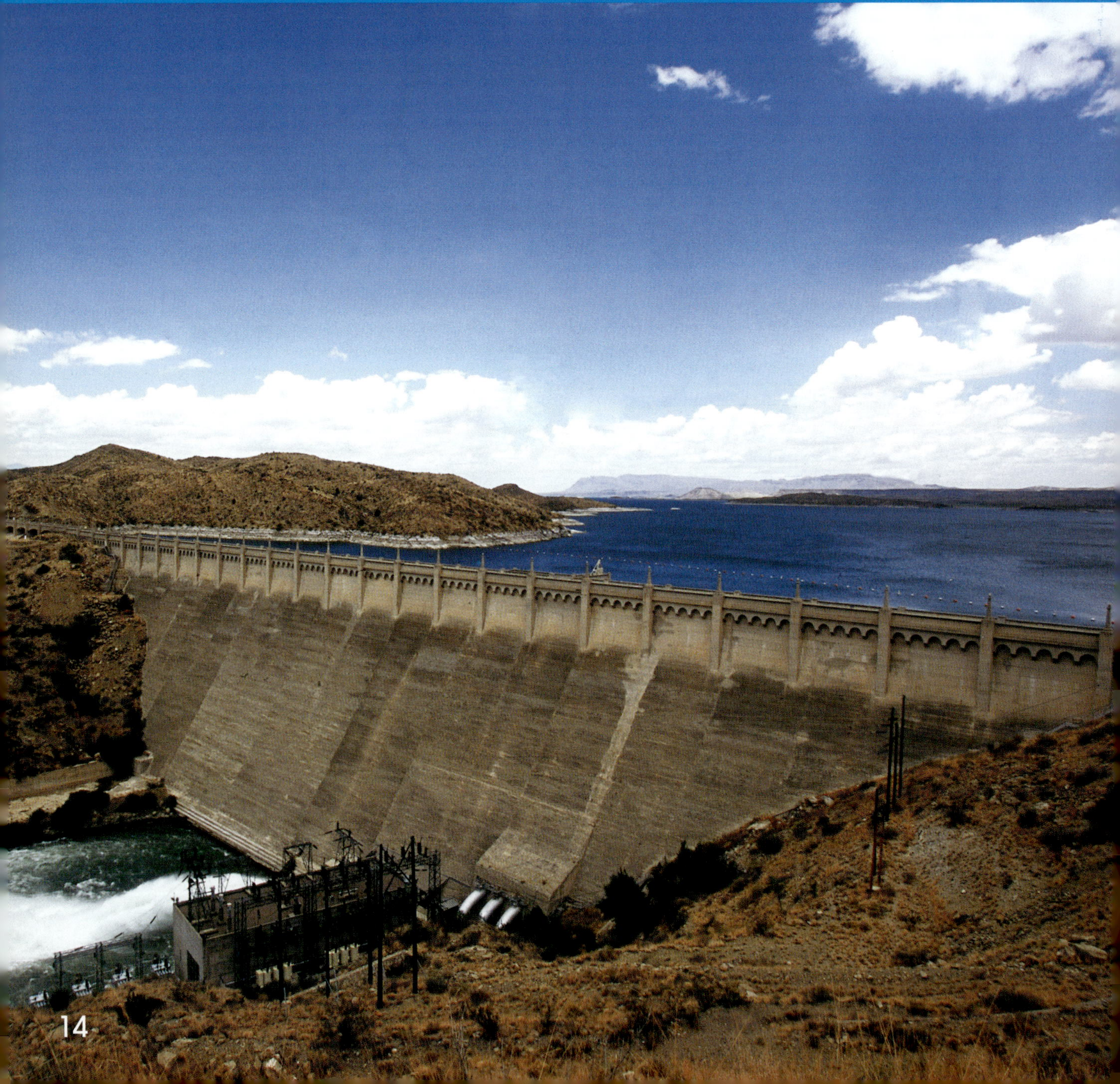

People Change Rivers

People change rivers by controlling the water's flow with **levees** and dams. Levees are built to make river banks higher and to try to control flooding. Dams block rivers and form lakes called reservoirs behind them. But dams can also block fish from finding food and stop water from reaching plants.

People ruin rivers by **polluting** them. Some people dump garbage and chemical waste into rivers. Pollution kills river plants and animals.

◀ New Mexico's Elephant Butte Dam blocks the Rio Grande River, forming the Elephant Butte Reservoir.

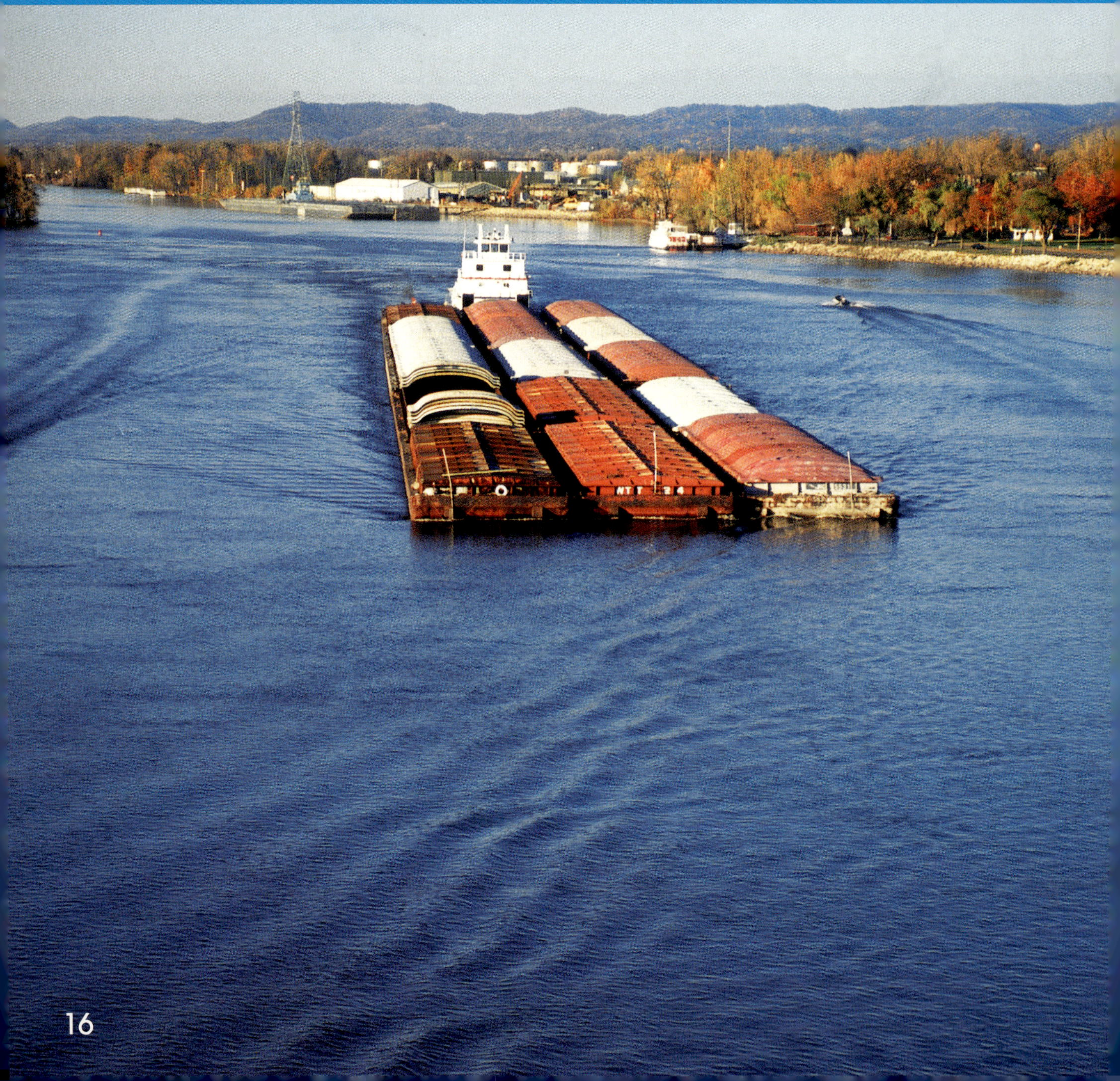

The Mississippi River

The Mississippi is the second longest river in North America at 2,350 miles (3,782 kilometers). The Mississippi River runs from Minnesota to the Gulf of Mexico.

For hundreds of years, people have shipped goods on the Mississippi River. At first, barges couldn't travel the whole river because of shallow areas. People added dams and **locks** to allow the barges to pass. Dams create steplike water levels on the river. Near dams, locks raise or lower barges to the water level created by dams.

◀ A barge moves along the Mississippi River. Barges move tons of coal on the river each year.

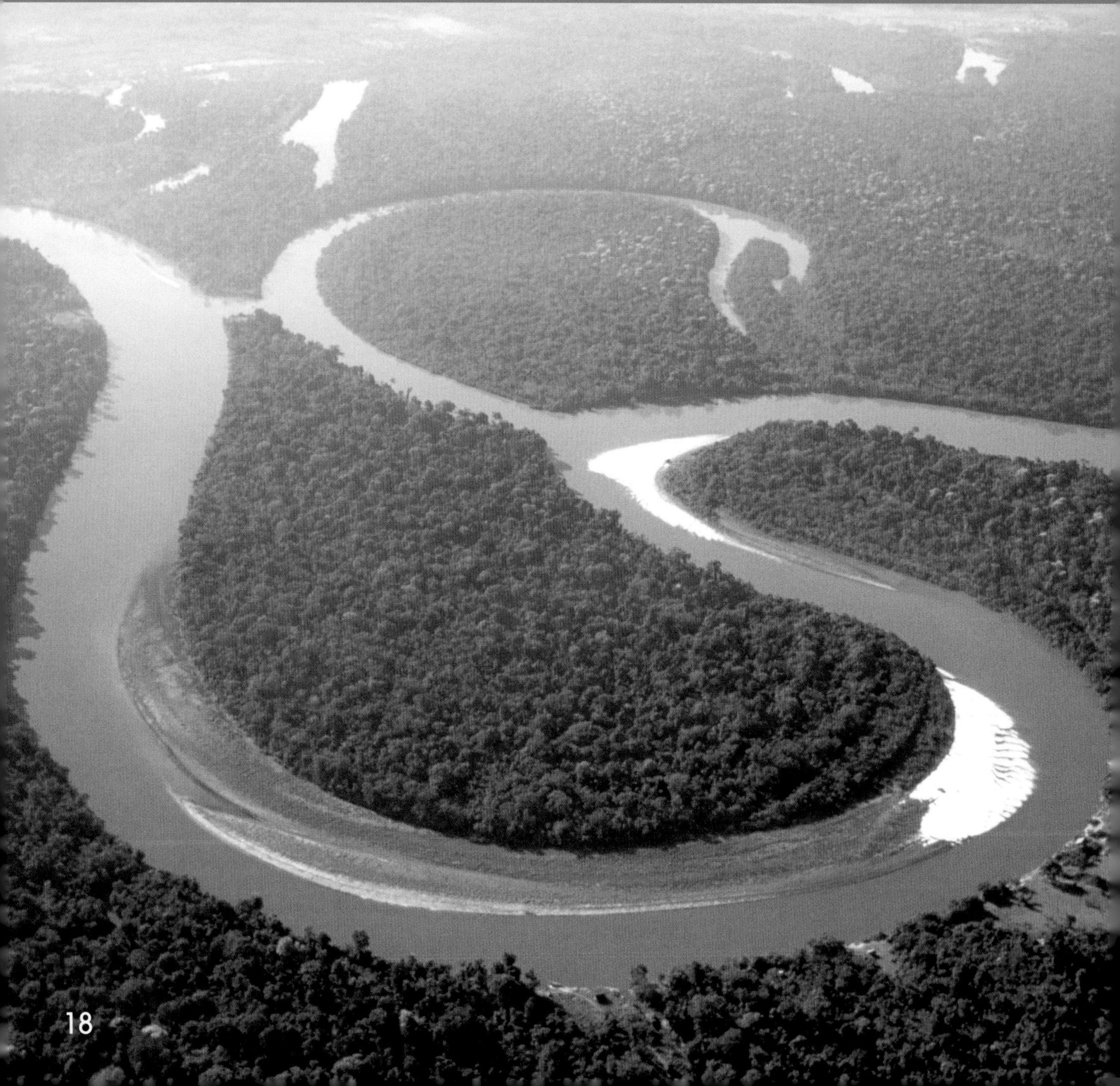

The Amazon River

South America's Amazon River holds more water than any river in the world. This wide river begins high in the Andes Mountains. It flows 4,000 miles (6,437 kilometers) to the Atlantic Ocean.

The Amazon is home to many unique animals. One of the largest freshwater fish in the world lives in these waters. Pirarucus can be 10 feet (3 meters) long. Poisonous freshwater stingrays swim along the river bottom. Pink dolphins whistle to each other as they jump above the Amazon's surface.

◄ Thick forests full of plants surround many miles of the curvy Amazon River.

LEGEND
City
River
UNITED STATES
Missouri River
Missouri River
Mississippi River
Mississippi River
Illinois River
Ohio River
Tennessee River
Arkansas River
MINNESOTA
WISCONSIN
IOWA
ILLINOIS
INDIANA
MISSOURI
KENTUCKY
TENNESSEE
ARKANSAS
MISSISSIPPI
LOUISIANA
St. Paul
Minneapolis
St. Louis
Memphis
New Orleans
N
S
E
W
SCALE
Kilometers
0 250 500
0 250 500
Miles

Rivers on a Map

Large and small rivers look like blue, curvy lines on a map. Large rivers have thick lines, while small rivers have thin lines. Rivers' names are beside the lines.

Look closer. Next to rivers you will find black dots for cities. For thousands of years, people have built homes and factories beside rivers. Each day people count on rivers to cool factory machines and ship goods. Now and in the future, rivers will continue to be an important part of daily life.

◀ Many rivers join to become part of the Mississippi River. Dots show cities that lie along this waterway.

Glossary

channel (CHAN-uhl)—a narrow stretch of water between two areas of land

climate (KLYE-mit)—the usual weather in a place

dam (DAM)—a barrier built across a river to hold back water

freshwater (FRESH-wa-tur)—water that has little or no salt

glacier (GLAY-shur)—a huge moving body of ice

levee (LEV-ee)—a bank built up near a river to try to control flooding

lock (LOK)—an area of water with gates at both ends

mouth (MOUTH)—the part of a river that empties into a lake or an ocean; the mouth is the end of a river.

pollute (puh-LOOT)—to make something dirty or unsafe

source (SORSS)—the place where a river begins

Read More

Graf, Mike. *The Amazon River.* Fact Finders. Land and Water. Mankato, Minn.: Capstone Press, 2004.

Royston, Angela. *Rivers.* My World of Geography. Chicago: Heinemann Library, 2005.

Internet Sites

FactHound offers a safe, fun way to find Internet sites related to this book. All of the sites on FactHound have been researched by our staff.

Here's how:
1. Visit *www.facthound.com*
2. Type in this special code **073685407X** for age-appropriate sites. Or enter a search word related to this book for a more general search.
3. Click on the **Fetch It** button.

FactHound will fetch the best sites for you!

Index

Amazon River, 19
animals, 11, 15, 19

barges, 17

channels, 5
climate, 9, 11
creeks, 5, 7

dams, 11, 15, 17

flood, 13, 15
formation, 7
freshwater, 5, 19

levees, 15
locks, 17

maps, 21
Mississippi River, 17, 21

Nile River, 11

parts of a river,
    banks, 5, 9, 11, 13, 15
    mouth, 5, 7
    source, 5, 7
people, 15, 17, 21
plants, 9, 15, 19
pollution, 15

reservoirs, 15

size, 5, 13, 17, 19, 21
streams, 5, 7

water speed, 5, 7, 13
water temperature, 9, 11
weather, 7, 13